Learning the
UNIX Operating System

Grace Todino and John Strang

Revised by Tim O'Reilly

O'Reilly & Associates, Inc.
103 Morris Street
Sebastopol, CA 95472

Learning the UNIX Operating System
by Grace Todino and John Strang

Editor: Tim O'Reilly

Printing History:

1986:	First edition written by Grace Todino and John Strang.
1987:	Second edition, revised by Tim O'Reilly.
April 1989:	Minor corrections.

ISBN: 0-937175-16-1   [12/91]

TABLE OF CONTENTS

1
Introduction

The UNIX Operating System

An *operating system* is a collection of programs that controls and organizes the resources of a computer system. These resources consist of hardware components such as terminals, printers and line printers, and the software programs that tell the computer to perform specific tasks.

Most personal computers have single-user operating systems. That is, only one person can use the system at a time, and the system can handle only one task at a time. Other operating systems are multi-user, multi-tasking systems; several terminals are connected to the computer and the operating system manages access to the computer by a community of users. This kind of operating system allows the computer to perform many functions at the same time.

UNIX is an operating system developed at Bell Laboratories. It is a multi-user, multi-tasking operating system. It also provides programs for editing text, sending electronic mail, preparing tables, performing calculations and many other specialized functions that normally require separate application programs.

UNIX is rapidly gaining support from such users as writers, scientists, programmers and managers who use and adapt UNIX to suit their specific needs. These needs might include:

- Text editing and printing
- Document handling and storage
- Programming and software development
- Electronic communication
- Computer-aided instruction
- Industrial process control
- Business administration

Versions of UNIX

There are many different versions of UNIX, the most important being AT&T's official release, known as System V, and the versions developed by the University of California at Berkeley, the latest of which is known as 4.3 bsd (Berkeley Standard Distribution).

Xenix, the most popular microcomputer implementation of UNIX, was originally based on an earlier AT&T release called Version 7, but has since been upgraded and made largely compatible with System V.

This handbook is oriented towards System V. However, in many cases, we comment on differences in Berkeley UNIX systems where we think the distinctions are particularly important to the user. You can use this handbook regardless of which type of system you have.

Very few implementations of UNIX are absolutely "pure" System V, so there may well be minor differences between what we present here and what happens on your system.

Scope of This Handbook

Learning the UNIX Operating System teaches the basic system utility commands to get you started with UNIX. We have carefully chosen the topics and commands that we feel a new user should learn. Our idea is not to overwhelm you with unnecessary details but to make you comfortable as soon as possible in the UNIX environment. We concentrate on the most basic and useful features of a command rather than detailing all the options it might have.

After reading this handbook, you should be able to perform the following tasks:

- ☐ Log in and log out of your system

- ☐ Use control keys to recover if you lose control of the system

- ☐ Send messages to other users on the system

- ☐ Manage UNIX files and directories, including listing, creating, copying, printing and removing files, and moving in and out of directories

- ☐ Work more efficiently using UNIX pipes, filters and multi-tasking

The Nutshell Format

The philosophy of this handbook is to give you a good overview of what we feel are UNIX survival materials for the new user. Learning a new operating system is often a daunting task, and we have made an effort to present concepts and commands in an easy-to-read and logical manner. The following sections describe the conventions used in this handbook.

Commands

You will find a brief introduction to a main concept before it is broken down into task-oriented sections. The appropriate command to use in each case is then presented, along with the function and use of the command and the proper syntax for using it. When the syntax is given, as in the following example:

rm *filename*

the items that you, as the user, would type in exactly as shown are printed in **boldface**. Items that are variable, for which you must supply your own value, are printed in *italics*. For example, the proper way to use the **rm** command is to type "rm" followed by the name of the file that you want to remove.

Examples

We have included several examples to show the results that you can
expect when you type in a command. The examples are not meant to
be typed in, as some of them assume that you have previously created
some files. If you do follow the examples, you may not get the same
results that we have shown.

Examples are set off from the main text in a constant-width typeface.
Items that you would enter if you were trying out the example are
shown in bold type. System messages and responses are printed in
normal type.

An example would appear as shown below:

```
$ lpt intro
lpt: command not found
$
```

The character "$" is the system prompt. You would type in "lpt
intro." The error message "lpt: command not found" is the system
response.

Problem Checklist

A problem checklist is included in those sections where you may run
into some trouble. You may skip these portions and go back to them
when you actually encounter a problem.

Exercises

You will find exercises in each section that will reinforce what you
have read in the text. Follow the exercises but do not be afraid to
experiment on your own.

The exercises are presented in two columns: the left-hand column tells
you what the command performs and the right-hand column tells you
to enter the words written in boldface. "Enter" means to type in the
words and then press the RETURN key.

For example, a line in the **Exercise** section on page 15 shows:

```
Find out today's date            Enter date
```

To follow the exercise, you type in the word **date** on your keyboard and then press the RETURN key. The first column tells you what will happen if you type in the **date** command.

After trying out the commands and seeing how your system responds to them, you will have a better idea of which commands to learn thoroughly. You can then look them up in the complete UNIX documentation package that comes with your system.

A Note To Our Readers

We see each Nutshell Handbook as reflecting the experience of a group of users. They're not written by "experts," but by people who have gone through a similar learning process as you. Our goal is to share what we know from experience so that you can become more productive in less time.

As publishers, this goal is reflected in the way we maintain the series by updating each title periodically. This allows us to incorporate changes suggested to us by our readers. We'd like new users to benefit from *your* experience as well as ours.

If you have a suggestion or solve a significant problem that our handbook does not cover, please write to us and let us know about it. Include information about the UNIX environment in which you work and the particular machine you use. If we are able to use your suggestion in the next edition of the book, we will send you a copy of the new edition. You'll have our thanks, along with thanks from future readers of this handbook.

2
Getting Started

Working in the UNIX Environment

Before you can start using UNIX and its facilities, the System Administrator has to set up a UNIX account for you. Think of this account as your office — it's your place in the UNIX environment. Other users may also be at work in UNIX.

Each user communicates with the computer from a terminal. To get into the UNIX environment you log in at your terminal. Logging in does two things: it identifies which user is at a specific terminal and it tells the computer that you are ready to begin working. When your work is finished, you log out and turn off your terminal.

Logging In

The process of making yourself known to the system and getting to your UNIX account is called *logging in*. Before you can start work, you must log in from a terminal and identify yourself. To log in, you type in your login ID (usually your name or initials) and a private password. The password does not appear on the screen as you type it in.

When you log in successfully, you will get some system messages and finally the UNIX system prompt. A successful login would look something like this:

```
O'Reilly & Associates, Inc.

login: john
password:
A handful of friends is worth more than a wagon of gold.
Thur  Nov 6  12:24:48  EST  1986
$
```

In this example, the system messages include a "fortune" and the date. The last line to appear is the UNIX system prompt. When you reach this point, you are successfully logged in to your account and can begin entering UNIX commands.

The messages that appear when you log in can be customized, so they might differ from system to system. The system prompt also differs. Throughout this book, we will use the prompt "$" in our examples.

The procedure to follow for logging in to UNIX is:

1. Turn on your terminal and press the ⌈RETURN⌉ key until the login prompt appears on the screen.

2. Type in your login ID in **lowercase letters** at the prompt. For example, if your login name is "john", type:

    ```
    login: john
    ```

    Press the ⌈RETURN⌉ key.

    The system should prompt you to enter your password. If passwords are not used on your system, you can skip the next step.

3. Type in your assigned password. Your password is not displayed on the screen as you type it.

    ```
    password:
    ```

    Press the ⌈RETURN⌉ key after you finish typing your password.

The system verifies your account name and password, and if they are correct, logs you in to your account.

Problem Checklist

√ *Nothing seemed to happen after I logged in.*

Wait for a minute, since the system may just be slow. If you still do not get anything, ask other users if they are having the same problem.

√ *The system says* "**login incorrect**".

Try logging in again, taking care to type in the correct name and password. If you still fail after logging in a few more times, check with the System Administrator to make sure you are using the right login ID and password for your account.

√ *All letters appear in* **UPPERCASE** *separated by backslashes.*

You must have typed your login name in uppercase. Type **logout** (**L\O\G\O\U\T**) and log in again.

The UNIX Shell

Once you've logged in, you're talking to a program called the shell. The shell interprets the commands that you type, invokes the various programs that you've asked for, and generally acts as a buffer between you and the UNIX operating system proper. There are two shells in common use: the Bourne shell and the Berkeley C shell.

The Bourne Shell is the standard UNIX shell. In this handbook, we assume that you are using this shell, because it is universally available. However, there are many advantages to using the C shell. These include the ability to review your previous commands, possibly editing them for current use, and the ability to program the shell to protect files from being accidentally lost or destroyed.

For a beginner, the difference between the two shells is slight. You can use this handbook with either shell, since we point out most of the significant differences in system operation with the C shell whenever they come up. However, you should ask your System Administrator which shell you are using.

If you plan on doing a lot of work in the UNIX environment you will want to learn more about the shell and its set of special commands. See Chapter 7 for pointers on where to look for more information.

The UNIX System Prompt

The system prompt is the shell's way of saying that it is ready and waiting for you to type in a command. When the system is finished running a command, the shell replies with a prompt to tell you that you can now type another command.

The Bourne shell uses $ as a system prompt. The C shell uses %. There are other shells and system prompts. Your own system prompt may be different from what we use here. The System Administrator may have set it up as a whole word (such as your name or your firm's name) rather than a single character. Your System Administrator can tell you how to customize or change the system prompt that appears on your screen.

Typing a Command

Typing a command at the UNIX system prompt tells the computer what to do. Your command identifies a UNIX program by name. When you press the RETURN key, the shell interprets your command and executes the program.

The first word that you type in is always a UNIX command. It is entered in lowercase. Some simple commands consist of a single lowercase word.

date

One example of a single-word command is **date**. When you enter the command **date**, the current date and time are displayed on your screen.

```
$ date
Thur  Nov  6  13:39  EST  1986
```

When you are typing a command line, the shell is simply collecting your input from the keyboard. Pressing the RETURN key tells the system that you have finished entering text and that it can start executing the command.

who

Another simple command is **who**. If you enter the command **who**, you can view a list of all the users that are currently logged in to the system. The listing also shows you the number of the terminal that they are working at and the time that they logged in.

There is a version of the **who** command that tells you who is logged in at the terminal you are using. The command line is **who am i**. This command line consists of the command (**who**) and an *argument* (**am i**).

```
$ who am i
john    tty4  Nov  6   08:26
$
```

The response shown in this example says that "I am" John, I am logged in at terminal 4 and that I logged in at 8:26 on the morning of November 6.

Correcting a Mistake

What do you do if you make a mistake in typing a command? Suppose you typed in "dare" instead of "date" and pressed the RETURN key before you realized your mistake. The shell will give you an error message.

```
$ dare
dare: command not found
$
```

Do not be overly concerned about getting error messages. Sometimes it may even appear that you typed the command correctly, but you still get an error message. Sometimes this can be caused by typing control characters that are invisible on the screen. Once the prompt returns, re-enter your command.

If you notice a typing mistake before pressing RETURN, you can backspace to erase the character and retype it.

The key used to perform this function differs from system to system and from account to account, and can be customized. The most common erase characters are:

- BACKSPACE key

- CTRL-H

- DELETE, DEL or RUBOUT key.

CTRL-H is called a *control character*. To type a control character (for example, CTRL-H), hold the CTRL key down while typing the letter "h". In the text, we will write control characters as CTRL-H, but in the examples, we will use the standard abbreviation: ^H. This is **not** the same as pressing the "^" (caret) key and then pressing the "h" key.

The key labeled DEL is often defined instead as the *interrupt character*. (It may be labeled DELETE or RUBOUT on some terminals.) This key is used to interrupt or cancel a command, and can be used anytime you want to quit what you are doing. Another key often programmed to do the same thing is CTRL-C.

Some other common control characters are:

CTRL-S   Pauses output from a program that is writing to the screen.

CTRL-Q   Restarts output after a pause by CTRL-S

CTRL-D   Returns you to UNIX command level. Used as end-of-file characters for some programs (like **cat** and **mail**). May also log you out of UNIX.

Find out the erase and interrupt characters for your account and write them down:

```
_____      Backspace and erase a character

_____      Interrupt a command
```

In Chapter 3, we'll tell you how to change these characters if you like.

Logging Out

Logging out is the process of ending a UNIX session. To log out, type the command **logout** followed by a RETURN. Unless you are using the C shell and have set the "ignoreeof" variable, pressing CTRL-D is another way to log out.

When you have successfully logged out, the login prompt should appear on the screen. This indicates that you are no longer logged into the system. You can then turn off your terminal or leave it on for the next user.

Problem Checklist

You are unlikely to experience any of the problems listed below in your first sessions with UNIX. These problems may occur later on, as you begin to do more advanced work.

√ *The system says* "**logout: not login shell.**"

You cannot log out because you are working in a subshell that was created by the original login shell. Press CTRL-D to return you to the original shell. If you are using the C shell, and "ignoreeof" has been set, you must type **exit**. You can now log out with the **logout** command.

√ *The system says* "**There are stopped jobs.**"

On Berkeley UNIX systems, the C shell supports a feature called job control that allows you to suspend programs temporarily while they are running. One or more of the programs you ran during your session has not ended but is instead in a paused state. If you don't care about your stopped jobs, type **logout** followed by a RETURN to immediately log out and kill the stopped jobs. Otherwise, type **fg** to bring the stopped job into the foreground. (See Chapter 6 for additional details.)

Syntax of UNIX Commands

UNIX commands can be simple, one-word entries like the **date** command. They can also be more complex in form and may require you to specify certain arguments. Unfortunately, there is no single convention for writing UNIX commands.

A UNIX command may or may not have an argument. An argument can be an option or a filename. The general format for UNIX commands is:

command *option(s) filename(s)*

While there is no single universal convention for writing UNIX commands and options, there is a definite UNIX style. The general rules are:

- Commands are entered in lower case.

- *Options* modify the way in which a command works. Options are often single letters prefixed with a minus (-) sign and set off by any number of spaces or tabs. If you make a mistake in specifying the options, some commands will display the allowable options.

- Multiple options in one command line can either be set off individually or combined after a single minus sign.

- The argument *filename* is the name of a file that you want to manipulate in some way. If you specify a filename incorrectly, you may get the response *"filename*: **no such file or directory"** or *"filename*: **cannot open"**.

- Spaces between commands, option(s) and filename(s) are important.

- Two commands can be written on the same line, separated by a semicolon (;) and written on the same command line. Commands entered in this way are executed sequentially by UNIX.

There are numerous commands available on the UNIX system. Do not try to memorize all of them. In fact, there is only a small body of commands and their options that you will find particularly useful for routine work. Gradually you will become familiar with these commands and how they can be modified to suit the particular type of work that you do. Some of the more useful UNIX commands are discussed in later chapters.

Let's look at an example of a UNIX command. The ls command displays a list of files. It can be used with or without arguments with slightly different results. If you enter:

```
$ ls
```

a list of filenames will be displayed on the screen. But if you enter:

```
$ ls -l
```

there will be an entire line of information for each file. The -l option modifies the normal output of the ls command and lists files in the *l*ong format. You can also ask for information about a particular file by adding a filename as a second argument. For example, to find out about a file called *chap1*, you would type:

```
$ ls -l chap1
```

When you want to specify multiple options, you can write the command in one of the following equivalent forms:

```
$ ls -a -l
$ ls -al
```

You must type a space after the command name and before the minus sign that introduces the options. If you type **ls-al**, the shell will say "**ls-al: command not found.**" Simply re-enter the correct form of the command at the system prompt.

Exercise: Entering a few commands

There is no better way to familiarize yourself with the UNIX environment than by entering a few commands. You should be logged into UNIX to begin this exercise. To execute a command, type in the command and then press the RETURN key. Remember that UNIX commands are always typed in lower case.

Find out today's date	Enter **date**
Find out logged in users	Enter **who**
Obtain more information about users	Enter **who -u**
Find out who is at your terminal	Enter **who am i**
Enter two commands in the same line	Enter **who am i;date**
Mistype a command	Enter **whom**

In this session, you have practiced several simple commands and viewed the results on the screen.

The Unresponsive Terminal

Other than making mistakes in typing a command, the only other problem you will most likely encounter during your UNIX session (the period that you are logged in) is a terminal that does not respond when you type a command. The terminal is said to be "hung."

There are several possible reasons why a terminal can be hung. The following solutions usually work and should be tried out in the order they are given until the system begins to respond.

1. Press the RETURN key.

    You may have typed a command but forgot to type RETURN to tell the shell that you are done typing and that it should begin interpreting the command.

    If you can type commands, but nothing happens when you press RETURN, try pressing LINE FEED or CTRL-J. If this works, your terminal needs to be reset so that carriage returns will again be recognized properly. (Some systems have a **reset** command that you can invoke by typing CTRL-J**reset**CTRL-J. If this doesn't work, you may need to log out and log back in, or turn your terminal on and off again.)

2. Press the DELETE key, or type CTRL-C two or three times. (Which key you use depends on the interrupt key defined for your account.)

   This interrupts a program that may be running. (Unless a program is run in the background, as described in Chapter 6, the shell will wait for it to finish before giving a new prompt. A long-running program may thus appear to hang the terminal.)

3. Type CTRL-Q .

   If output has been stopped with CTRL-S, this will restart it. (Note that some programs will automatically issue CTRL-S if they need to pause output; this character may not have been entered from the keyboard.)

4. Check that the NO SCROLL key is not locked or toggled on.

   This key stops the screen display from being scrolled upwards when the cursor has reached the bottom line. If your keyboard has a NO SCROLL key that can be toggled on and off, keep track of whether you have pressed it an odd or even number of times when you try to free yourself.

5. Check the physical connection to the terminal and from the terminal to the system.

6. Type CTRL-D .

   Some programs (like **mail**) expect text from the user. If so, they may be waiting for an end-of-file character from you to tell them that the entered text is finished. Typing CTRL-D may cause you to log out, so you should try this as a last resort.

7. Turn your terminal off and on again. (This may log you out.)

If none of these work, turn to a local system expert for help and watch carefully.

3
Your UNIX Account

Once you log in, you can begin to use the many facilities UNIX provides. Your starting point is your login account:

- A place in the UNIX file system where you can store your files.

- A login id that identifies you uniquely, allowing you to control access to your files, and to receive mail from other users.

- A customizable environment that you can tailor to your liking.

The UNIX File System

A *file* is the unit of storage in UNIX, as in many other systems. A file can contain anything: a program, executable object code, text, and so on — all are just sequences of raw data until they are interpreted by the right program.

In UNIX, files are organized into directories. A *directory* is actually a file which contains information for the system to use to find other files. A directory can be thought of as a place, so that files are said to be contained *in* directories and you are said to work *inside* a directory.

The Directory Tree

The directories are organized into a hierarchical structure that is usually imagined as an upside-down family tree. The parent directory of the tree is known as the *root* and is written (by convention) as a slash (/).

The root contains several directories. Let us expand the tree and see what directories are contained in root:

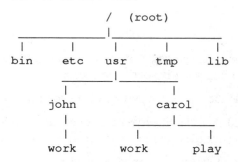

Figure 1. Example of a Directory Tree

bin, *etc*, *usr*, *tmp* and *lib* are subdirectories of root. These are fairly standard directories and usually contain specific kinds of system files. For instance, *bin* contains many UNIX commands.

In our example, the directory *usr* has a parent directory *root* that lies one level above. It also has two child directories *john* and *carol* that lie directly one level below. Each directory has one parent directory and may have one or more child directories. The child directories (like *carol*) may have child directories themselves (like *work* and *play*), to a limitless depth for practical purposes.

The notation used to specify file and directory names is called a *pathname*. A pathname is similar to an address and locates the position of the directory or file in the UNIX file system.

Absolute Pathnames

The UNIX file system organizes the files and directories in an inverted tree structure with the parent directory or the *root* at the top. An absolute pathname tells you the path of directories you must travel to get from the root to where you want to go.

For example, */usr/john* is an absolute pathname and defines a unique directory as follows:

- the root is designated by "*/*"
- the directory *usr* (a directory of *root*)
- the directory *john* (a subdirectory of *usr*)

This structure is shown in the figure below:

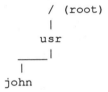

Figure 2. Path of Directory "john"

If you look at Figure 1 on the previous page, you will see that the directory *john* has a child directory named *work*. Its absolute pathname is */usr/john/work*. One directory in Carol's account has the same name, but it is a different directory. Its absolute pathname is */usr/carol/work*.

The root is always indicated by the first slash (*/*) in the pathname.

Relative Pathnames

Another way of writing the address of a file or directory is to use a *relative pathname*. A relative pathname points to a file relative to your current working directory.

Unless you specify an absolute pathname, the shell assumes you are using a relative pathname. Relative pathnames can go through more than one directory level by naming the directories along the path.

You can go up the tree by using the shorthand ".." (dot dot) for the parent directory. You can also go down the tree by specifying directory names. You just name each step along the way, separated by a slash (/).

Using our directory tree example, if the current directory is */usr/john*, the relative pathname to *work* is simply *work* since you are already in the correct directory. Note that you do not start with a "/", as this would specify an absolute address relative to the root.

In order to get to the *play* subdirectory of *carol* when you are in *john*, you may use the absolute pathname */usr/carol/play*. Alternatively, you can go up one level (using the ".." notation) to *usr*, then go down the tree to *carol* and finally to *play*. This is shown in the following figure:

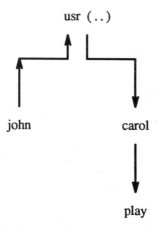

usr (..)

john   carol

play

The relative pathname would be *../carol/play*. It is wrong to give the relative address as *carol/play*. This form implies that *carol* is a child directory of */usr/john*.

Absolute and relative pathnames are totally interchangeable. UNIX commands simply follow whatever path you specify to wherever it leads. If you use an absolute pathname, the path starts from the root. If you use a relative pathname, the path starts from your current directory. Choose whichever is easier at the moment. You can even backtrack over the path using **cd ..**, as will be described later.

Your Home Directory

When you log in to UNIX, you enter a unique directory called your *home directory*. This home directory contains the files you use almost every time you log in. Your home directory is a unique place in the UNIX file system from which you can create your own files and build your own directory tree.

Your Working Directory

Your *working directory* is the directory you are currently in. At the start of every session, your home directory is your working directory. You may change to another directory, in which case the directory you transferred to becomes your current working directory.

All commands that you enter apply to the files in your current working directory. When you create files, they are created in your working directory.

pwd

To find out what directory you are currently in, use the **pwd** (*print working directory*) command. The **pwd** command takes no arguments.

```
$ pwd
/usr/john
$
```

Each filename or directory name follows its parent directory and is separated from it by a slash (/). In this way, each child directory or subdirectory follows its parent.

Changing Directories

When you know the absolute or relative pathname of a file or directory, you can move up and down the UNIX directory tree.

cd

You can change your working directory to a parent or child directory or to another user's directory with the **cd** (*change directory*) command.

The **cd** command has the form:

>   **cd** *pathname*

The argument *pathname* can be an absolute or a relative pathname to the directory you want to change to. Use the form that is most convenient for you at that time.

```
$ cd /usr/carol
$ pwd
/usr/carol
$ cd work
$ pwd
/usr/carol/work
$
```

The single-word command **cd**, with no arguments, will always take you back to your home directory, wherever you may be in the file system.

Note that you can only change to another directory. You cannot **cd** to a filename, or UNIX will give you an error message.

```
$ cd /etc/passwd
/etc/passwd: Not a directory
$
```

/etc/passwd is a file that contains the names of users allowed to log in to the system.

Listing Files

In order to use the **cd** command, you must find out, in a directory, which of its entries are subdirectories and which are files. The **ls** command is used to list the files in the directory tree.

ls

When you enter the **ls** command, you will get a listing of the files and subdirectories contained in your working directory. The syntax is simple:

> **ls** *option(s) filename(s)*

If you've just logged in for the first time, entering **ls** without any arguments may not appear to do anything. This is not surprising, since you have not yet created any files in your working directory. If you have no files, nothing is displayed and you will simply get a new system prompt.

```
$ ls
$
```

But if you have previously created some files in your account, those filenames are displayed. The output you get will depend on the files you have in the directory. However, the display should look something like this:

```
$ ls
ch1
ch10
ch2
ch3
intro
$
```

There are a number of different options that **ls** can take to display different amounts of information related to files and directories as well as to change the format of the display. If you would rather display files alphabetically in columns, use the -*x* option:

```
$ ls -x
ch1    ch10    ch2    ch3    intro
```

(On Berkeley UNIX systems, **ls** displays files in columns like this by default.)

The *-a* option (for *a*ll) is guaranteed to show you some more files, as in the following example:

```
$ ls -ax
.           .exrc     ch1       ch2       intro
..          .profile  ch10      ch3
$
```

At least two new files have appeared, with the names "." (dot) and ".." (dot dot). As mentioned earlier, .. is a special notation for the parent directory. A single . is a special notation for the current directory. There may also be other files, like *.profile* or *.exrc*. Any file whose name begins with a dot is hidden—it will only be listed if you type **ls -a**. (*.profile* contains commands that are automatically executed by the Bourne shell whenever you log in. The C shell uses the two files *.login* and *.cshrc* instead of *.profile*. *.exrc* contains commands that are automatically executed by the **ex** or **vi** editors whenever you start either one.)

To get more information about each file, add the **-l** option. This option can be used alone, or in combination with **-a**, as shown here.

```
$ ls -al
total 94
drwxr-xr-x  2 john   doc     512 Jul 10 22:25 .
drwxr-xr-x  4 bin    bin    1024 Jul  8 11:48 ..
-rw-r--r--  1 john   doc     136 Jul  8 14.46 .exrc
-rw-r--r--  1 john   doc     833 Jul  8 14:51 .profile
-rw-rw-rw-  1 john   doc   31273 Jul 10 22:25 ch1
-rw-rw-rw-  1 john   doc       0 Jul 10 21:57 ch2
 |    |     |   |     |     |        |            |
 | access  | owner   |     |  creation date      |
 | modes   |       group   |    and time         |
type      # of           # bytes            filename
          links

$
```

The long format provides the following information about each file:

total *n*	*n* number of 1024-byte blocks of storage used by the files in this directory
type	Tells whether the file is a directory (*d*) or a plain file (-)
access mode	Specifies three types of users (yourself, your group, all others) who are allowed to read (*r*), write (*w*), or execute (*x*) your files
links	The number of files and directories linked to the file
owner	Who created or owns the file
group	The group that owns the file
# bytes	The size of the file
creation date	When the file was last modified
filename	Name of the file or directory

Notice especially the columns that list the owner and group of the files, and the access modes, or permissions. The person who creates a file is its owner; if you've created any files, this column should show your login id. You also belong to a group, to which you were assigned by the System Administrator. Any files you create will be marked with the name of your group.

The permissions control who can read, write (modify) or execute the file (if it is a program). There are a total of ten characters in the permissions listing. The first character shows the file type (directory or plain file). The next three characters show the permissions for the file's owner—you if you created the file. The next three characters show permissions for other members of your group. The final three characters show permissions for all other users.

For example, the permissions for *.profile* are **-rw-r--r--**, meaning that it is a plain file, that you, the owner have both read and write permissions, but that other users of the system can only read the file; they cannot modify it.

In the case of directories, **x** means the permission to search the directory—for example, to list its contents with **ls**. Notice that the two directories shown in the example are executable (searchable by you, by your group, and by everyone else on the system).

You can use the **chmod** command to change the permissions of your files. See your UNIX documentation for details.

If you are interested only in knowing which files are directories and which are executable files, you can list the files using the -**F** option.

```
$ ls -Fx /usr/john
calendar    goals       ideas/
ch2         guide/      test*
$
```

Directories are marked with / (slash) at the end of the filename. In our example, the files *ideas* and *guide* are directories. You can verify this by listing the files with the -*l* option and noting the "d" in the first field of the output. Files with an execute status (x), like programs and shell scripts, are marked with a * (star). The file *test* is an executable file. Files that are not marked are not executable.

Exercise: Exploring the File System

You are now equipped to explore the file system with **cd**, **ls**, and **pwd**. Try a few **cd** commands interspersed with **pwd** commands. Take a tour of the directory system, hopping many steps at a time. (Note: The form **ls** *dirname* lists files in the directory called *dirname*).

Go to your home directory	Enter **cd**
Find out your working directory	Enter **pwd**
Change to new working directory	Enter **cd /etc**
List files in new working directory	Enter **ls**
Change directory to root and list files	Enter **cd /; ls**
Change to a new directory with relative pathname	Enter **cd usr**
Give a wrong pathname	Enter **cd etc**

Change to a new directory with absolute pathname	Enter **cd /etc**
Find out working directory	Enter **pwd**
List files in another directory	Enter **ls /bin**
Return to home directory	Enter **cd**

Looking Inside Files

By now, you're probably tired of looking at files from the outside. It's kind of like going to a bookstore and looking at the covers, but never getting to read a word. Let's look at three programs for reading files: **cat**, **pg** and **more**.

cat

Most first-time users of UNIX think that **cat** is a strange name for a program. **cat** is actually short for "concatenate" and, as we'll see later, is used to put files together (to concatenate files) in order to create a bigger file. It can also be used to print a file to the terminal screen.

To display a file on the standard output, use:

cat *filename*

For example, let's display the contents of the file */etc/passwd*. This file contains the names of users who have accounts, and is used by the system each time you log in.

```
$ cat /etc/passwd
root::0:0:Root:/:/bin/sh
daemon:NONE:1:1:Admin:/:
      .
      .
      .
```

$

cat works best for short files containing 24 lines (or one screenful) or less. If you **cat** a file that is too long, it may roll up the screen faster than you can read it. Press CTRL-S to freeze the output at a particular point. Press CTRL-Q key to resume listing the file. You cannot go back to view the previous screens when you use **cat**.

If you accidentally or inquisitively type **cat** without a filename, press CTRL-D to get out of **cat**.

pg

If you want to "read" a long file on the screen, you can use the **pg** (for "*page*") command to display one screen or "page" of text at a time. A screen can usually display 24 lines of text, depending on how your terminal is set up. The syntax is:

pg *file*

pg allows you to move *forward or backward* in the files by any number of pages or lines, and to specific pages or lines, just as if you were reading a printed copy of the file. You can also move back and forth between two or more files, specified on the command line. When you invoke **pg**, the first "page" of the file appears on the screen. A colon (:) appears at the bottom of the screen, as in the following example:

```
$ pg ch03
A file is the unit of storage in UNIX, as in many
other systems.  A file can be anything:  a program,
                        .
                        .
                        .

:
```

The colon is a signal for you to enter a **pg** command to tell it what to do. Press the RETURN key to view the next page. At the last page, the end of the file is marked by the prompt "**(EOF):**". Pressing RETURN once more will get you to the UNIX prompt.

You can enter "**h**" (for "*h*elp") at the **pg** prompt to display the **pg** commands available on your system. Some of the simpler, but quite useful ones are given in the table below.

Table 3-1
Useful pg Commands

Command	Description
l or -l	Display one more line at bottom or top (letter "l", not number)
xl	Begin page at line *x*
RETURN	Display next page
n	Move to page *n*
+ or -*n*	Move forward or backward by *n* pages
d	Display half a page more
.	Redisplay current page
f	Skip next page
$	Go to last page.
h	Help
n	Go to next file
p	Go back to previous file
q	Quit out of **pg**

The following example shows how **pg** breaks up a file into a sequence of pages and allows you to move to specific pages. We invoke **pg** with the *-p* option to change the colon prompt so that it includes the current page number (%**d**) within brackets. The syntax is:

    pg -p "[%**d**]:" *file*

Displaying the page number helps you keep track of where you are as you move forward and backward through the file. While this is obviously too much to type on the command line, it is useful for our demonstration. When you learn more about shell programming, you will discover simple ways to create your own version of the **pg** command that includes this option. Note that the *-p* option is invoked when you enter **pg** at the command line, and is not the same as the *p* command entered at the colon prompt.

```
$ pg -p "[%d]:" ch03
A file is a unit of storage in UNIX, as in many
other systems.  A file can be anything:  a program,
```

```
executable object code, text
                    .
                    .
                    .
[1]: +3

skipping ahead

the directory usr (a directory of root)
the directory john ( a subdirectory of usr)
                    .
                    .
                    .
[4]:
```

In the above example, the prompt "[1]:" says that you are looking at "page 1" of the file. We enter the command to move three pages forward (+3), and the system displays the message "**Skipping ahead**". The next screen shows that the page number has been updated to "[4]:". You could have also moved to the fourth page by entering "**4**". Remember that a screen-sized page does **not** correspond to a printed page.

more

The **pg** command is not available on Berkeley UNIX systems, although it is a very useful command for reading files on the terminal. Berkeley systems have the **more** command instead. It works just like **pg** but has different features. For example, **more** does not allow you to move backward through a file or to specific lines. However, it lets you enter the **vi** editor at the point in the file that you are currently scanning. **more** is also called **page** on some systems.

The format of the command is:

    more *filename*

If your system has **more**, try it out on a moderately-sized file of 30 or more lines. Your screen displays the first page of the file. The last line is a "percentage seen" message like:

```
(More) --- 47%
```

This says that you are *47%* of your way through the file. Press SPACE BAR to view the next page. Enter "**h**" to see what commands are available with **more**.

Communicating with Other Users

We've seen that each file is marked with its owner's login id. An even more visible sign that the system knows each of its users by name is that you can communicate with other users via electronic mail.

When you log in to your system, you may get a message that says "You have mail." Someone in the network of UNIX users has sent you a message or document through the mail. This facility allows you to compose a message at your terminal and send it to another user or list of users. It also enables you to read any messages that others may have sent to you.

The UNIX **mail** program has three advantages over paper mail: it is convenient if you are already logged in, it is delivered instantly, and both you and the recipient can store messages in the file system for reference.

Sending Mail

When you send mail to another user, the recipient does not have to be logged in. The messages you send are stored in the recipient's "mailbox," a file deep in the UNIX file system (often located in the directory */usr/mail*). They are kept there until the recipient logs in and decides to read them.

To send mail to another user, give the user name of the person(s) to whom you want to send a message, as in the following:

    mail *user1 user2* ...

The System V **mail** program will *not* give you a prompt when you enter this command. Instead, **mail** is waiting for you to enter your message. (On Berkeley UNIX systems, the **mail** program will first prompt you for the subject of the message.) Type in your message and press the [RETURN] key after every line, just as you would on a typewriter. When you have finished entering text, enter [CTRL-D] on a separate line. You should get the system prompt at this point. You can get out of the **mail** program while you are still entering text with the [DEL] key or [CTRL-C] (or whatever other interrupt key is defined for your account). The interrupted message is placed in a file called **dead.letter** in your working directory.

```
$ mail carol
How about dinner tonight?
^D
$
```

If you change your mind about inviting Carol to dinner, you will have to send her another message since you cannot cancel a message once you have pressed [CTRL-D] .

Reading Your Mail

In order to read your mail, simply enter **mail** at the system prompt. You can do this any time during the UNIX session, not just when you log in.

Let's read John's message to Carol:

```
$ mail
From john   Thur   Nov   6    13:42
How about dinner tonight?

?
```

The output of **mail** says that the message was sent by *john* on Thursday, November 6, at 1:42 pm. The question mark ("?") on the last line is the **mail** program prompt. Just as the UNIX system prompt is a sign that the shell is waiting for you to enter a command, the **mail** prompt is a sign that the mail program is waiting for you to enter a **mail** command. Your **mail** prompt may consist of a single character. Find out the **mail** prompt on your system. Then enter one of the commands in the following table.

Table 3-2
Mail Commands

Command	Description
?	Display menu of **mail** commands
SPACE BAR	Display the next message. Also, "+".
-	Display previous message
p	Display message again
d	Delete the message and go on to the next. If you don't delete the message, it will be displayed again each time you invoke **mail**.
m *users*	Forward a message you have received to the named user(s)
s *file*	Save a message in the named file
x	Exit the **mail** program, restoring any messages you have deleted.
q	Quit the **mail** program.

The first mail that you read is the one that was last sent to you; mail messages are displayed first-in, last-out. If you want to read the first message first, use the **-r** option of **mail**.

The Berkeley version of **mail** doesn't start out by printing your messages. Instead, it prints a "message header" that lists whether each message is "new" (*N*) or "unread" (*U*), a message number, the sender, and when the message was sent. The current message is marked by ">".

```
$ mail
> U  1  john  Fri  Aug 30  13:42
  N  2  carol Fri  Aug 30  15:25
mail?
```

You can choose the message you want to read by entering the message number at the **mail** prompt. Once the mail message is read, it is automatically moved to a file called *mbox* in the user's home directory. This version of **mail** has more options and features than the System V **mail** program described earlier. System V users are not out of luck, though. It is available under the name of **mailx** in many System V installations.

You can practice sending mail to your friends in this exercise. List the users logged on to the system and choose a name. You can also use your user name to send mail to yourself. Enter the following message. Do not forget to press the ⎡RETURN⎤ key after typing in a line, and type ⎡CTRL-D⎤ on a line by itself when you're done.

```
List logged on users    Enter who

Send mail to someone     Enter mail name
                         Hi there! I am just
                         trying out how to
                         send mail.
                         ^D
```

Customizing Your Account

As we saw earlier, your home directory includes a hidden file called *.profile* (*.login* and *.cshrc* if you are using the C shell). This file is the key to customizing your account, since it contains commands that are automatically executed whenever you log in.

Let's take a look at this file. Return to your home directory and display the file using **cat**. Your *.profile* might look something like this:

```
/usr/games/fortune
date
PATH=.:/bin:/usr/bin:/usr/local/bin;export PATH
umask 002
stty erase ^H intr ^C
```

As you can see, the *.profile* contains commands to print a "fortune" and the date—just what happened earlier when we logged in! (**/usr/games/fortune** is a useless but entertaining program that prints a randomly selected line from its collection of aphorisms. It may not be available on all systems.)

But what are these other commands?

- The line beginning **PATH**= gives the shell a list of directories in which to look for commands. This saves you the trouble of typing the complete pathname for each program you want to run. (Notice that */usr/games* isn't part of the path, and so we must use the full pathname to receive our daily dose of wisdom.)

- The **umask** command sets the default file permissions that will be assigned to all files that you create. Without going into the complexities of this command, let it suffice to say that a value of 022 will produce the permissions **rw-r--r--** (read-write by owner, but read-only by everyone else), and 002 will produce **rw-rw-r--** (read-write by owner and group, but read-only by everyone else). See your UNIX documentation for details.

- The **stty** command sets your terminal control characters—for example, the erase and interrupt characters we discussed earlier.

You can execute any of these commands from the command line as well. For example, to change your erase character from BACKSPACE (CTRL-H) to DEL (CTRL-?), you would type:

```
$ stty erase ^?
```

(The DEL key actually generates the control code CTRL-?, so that is what you will see on your screen, even if you press DEL.)

Now, pressing DEL will backspace and erase characters you type. (If your account is already set up to use DEL as the erase character, reverse this example, and change the erase character to BACKSPACE.)

If you experiment with **stty**, you should be careful not to reset the erase or interrupt character to a character you'll need otherwise.

Just as you can execute the commands in *.profile* from the command line, the converse is true: any non-interactive command that you can execute from the command line can be executed automatically when you log in by placing it in your *.profile*.

It is premature at this point for you to edit your *.profile*, but it is good to know what it contains. Later, when you know more about the UNIX environment, feel free to add or change commands in this file.

4
File Management

Methods of Creating Files

Normally you would create a text file with a text editor. An editor combines the power of a typewriter, an erasable pencil on paper, scissors, and paste. The usual editors in the UNIX environment are **vi** (pronounced "vee-eye") and **ed**.

ed is a line-based editor that is on virtually all UNIX systems. It allows you to modify files on a line-by-line basis.

vi is a screen editor that allows you to move a cursor around the screen to get to the line or word that you want to modify.

Many UNIX systems also now support easy-to-use word processors. Check with your System Administrator for availability.

Since several edit programs are available, you can choose to edit with the editor you feel comfortable with. **vi** is probably the best choice, since it is available on almost all UNIX systems. Another Nutshell Handbook, *Learning the Vi Editor*, describes **vi** in detail.

You can also create a file by using a UNIX feature called *input/output redirection*, as described in the next chapter. The output of a command can be sent directly to a file, thus creating a new file or a larger file out of many smaller files.

Wildcards in File Names

A *filename* is the most important property of a file. Filenames may contain any character except /, which is reserved as the separator between files and directories in a pathname. Filenames are usually are made up of upper and lower case letters, numbers, and the special characters "." (dot) and "_" (underscore). In System V, filenames can be up to 14 characters long. Berkeley UNIX systems allow longer filenames.

A *filename* must be unique inside its directory, but there may be other files in other directories with the same names. For example, you may have the files called *chap1* and *chap2* in the directory */usr/carol/work* and also have files with the same names in */usr/carol/play*.

When you have a number of files named in series (for example, *chap1* to *chap12*) or filenames with common characters (like *aegis*, *aeon* and *aerie*), you can use *wildcards* (also called *metacharacters*) to specify many files at once. These special characters are * and ?. When used in a filename given as an argument to a command:

* is replaced by any number of characters in a filename. For example, *ae** would match *aegis*, *aerie*, *aeon*, etc. if they were in the same working directory. You can use this to save typing for a single filename (for example, *al** for *alphabet.txt*) or to name many files at once (as in *ae**.)

? is replaced by any **single** character (so *h?p* matches *hop* and *hip*, but not *help*).

In addition, you can use brackets ([ ]) to surround a choice of characters you'd like to match. Any *one* of the characters between the brackets will be matched. For example, *[Cc]hapter* would match either *Chapter* or *chapter* (but *[ch]apter* would match either *capter* or *hapter*). Use a hyphen to separate a range of consecutive characters. For example, *chap[1-3]* would match either *chap1*, *chap2*, or *chap3*.

The examples below demonstrate the use of wildcards.

```
$ ls -x
chap10      chap2       chap5       chap9
chap1a.old  chap3.old   chap6       haha
chap1b      chap4       chap7
```

```
$ ls -x chap?
chap2      chap5      chap7
chap4      chap6      chap9
$ ls -x chap[5-7]
chap5      chap6      chap7
$ ls -x chap1?
chap10     chap1b
$ ls -x *.old
chap1a.old      chap3.old
$ ls -x *a*a
chap1a.old      haha
```

Wildcards are useful for more than listing files. Most commands take more than one filename, and you can use wildcards to specify multiple files in the command line. For example, the command **pg** is used to display a file on the screen. Let's say you want to display files *chap3.old* and *chap1a.old*. Instead of specifying these files individually, you could enter the command as:

```
$ pg *old
$
```

This is equivalent to "**pg chap1a.old chap3.old**".

Managing Your Files

The hierarchical tree structure of the UNIX file system makes it easy for you to organize and arrange your files. After creating and modifying files for some time, you may find that you have to copy or move files from one directory to another, rename files to distinguish different versions of a file or give several names to the same file. In fact, you may have to create new directories each time you start working on a different project.

A directory tree can easily get cluttered with files containing old and unnecessary information. When you no longer need a file or a directory, it is good practice to delete these files in order to free up storage space on your disk.

Copying Files

It is sometimes useful to make a copy of a file when you want to modify it so that the contents of the original file are not lost.

cp

The **cp** command is used to copy a file in the same directory or to copy a file to and from directories. **cp** does not destroy the original file so it is a useful way of maintaining an identical backup of a file.

To make a copy of the file, use the command:

> **cp** *old new*

where *old* is a pathname to the original file and *new* is the name you want to give to the copy of the file. For example, to copy the */etc/passwd* file into a file called *password* in your working directory, you would enter:

```
$ cp /etc/passwd password
$
```

You can also use the form:

> **cp** *old old_dir*

This puts a copy of the original file *old* into an existing directory *old_dir*. It gives the name of the original file to the copy of the file.

You can copy more than one file at a time to a single directory by listing the name of each file you want copied, with the destination directory at the end of the command line. You can use relative or absolute pathnames as well as simple filenames. For example, if your current directory was */usr/carol*, to copy two files called *chap1* and *chap2* from */usr/john* to a subdirectory called *work*, you could enter:

```
$ cp ../john/chap1 ../john/chap2 work
$
```

Or, you could use wildcards and let the shell find all the appropriate files.

```
$ cp ../john/chap[1-2] work
```

You can also use the shorthand forms . and .. to refer to the current directory or its parent as the destination of the copy. For example:

```
$  cp ../john/chap[1-2] .
```

will copy the specified files to the current working directory.

Problem Checklist

√ *The system says "*cp: cannot copy file to itself.*"*

The copy of the file must be given a unique filename for that directory.

√ *The system says "*cp: *filename*: no such file or directory.*"*

The system cannot find the file that you want to copy. Check for a typing mistake. Also remember to specify the pathname of any file not in the current working directory.

√ *The system says something like "*cp: permission denied.*"*

You may not have permission to copy a file created by someone else or into a directory that does not belong to you. Use **ls -l** to find out the owner and the permissions for the file. If you feel that you should have permission to copy a file whose access is denied to you, ask the file's owner or the System Administrator to change the access modes for the file.

Renaming and Moving Files

You will sometimes need to change the name of a file when you have made a lot of changes to it or to set a copy apart from the original file. In order to rename a file, use the **mv** (*move*) command. The **mv** command is also used to actually move a file from one directory to another.

mv

The **mv** command has exactly the same syntax as the **cp** command:

>   **mv** *old new*

where *old* is the old name of the file and *new* is the new name that you want to give to it. It is always a good practice to make sure that the new name is unique; an existing file may be overwritten by the **mv** operation.

```
$ mv chap1 intro
$
```

The file *chap1* is "moved" to a new file called *intro*. If you list your files with **ls**, you will see that the file *chap1* has disappeared.

The **mv** command can also be used to actually move a file from one directory to another directory. As with the **cp** command, if the destination file is to have the same name as the file you want to move, then only the name of the destination directory need be supplied.

Linking Files

When you use the command **cp**, you create two copies of a file. The changes made to one file do not affect the other. In UNIX, you can also refer to a single file under different names in different directories. This is a feature of UNIX that allows you to link files instead of duplicating them.

ln

The **ln** (for *link*) command is used to make a file available from a different directory. It is also useful for giving multiple names to the same command file. A new copy of the file is not created when the **ln** command is used.

The format of the command is:

>   **ln** *filename othername*

The file can be referenced using either *filename* or *othername*. For example, if you are working on some portion of a large file together with another user, you may want to give a different name to the file. When you use the **ln** command to link the files, both names are equally valid and will reference the same file.

Creating Directories

It is usually more convenient to put all files related to one topic in the same directory. If you were writing a spy novel, you probably would not want your files containing your ideas mixed up with phone listings for restaurants. You would create two directories; one for all the chapters on your novel (*spy*, for example), and another for restaurants (*boston.dine*). Putting related files into one directory makes your own file system more structured and organized.

mkdir

In order to create a new directory, use the **mkdir** command. The format is:

> **mkdir** *dirname*

where *dirname* is the name of the new directory. To continue our example, you would enter:

```
$ mkdir spy
$ mkdir boston.dine
```

Removing Files and Directories

There will come a time when you no longer need a file or a directory. You may have already finished working on it and see no need to keep it on your file system. Or, the contents of the file may simply have become obsolete. It is good practice to periodically remove unwanted files and directories in order to free up some storage space on your disk.

rm

The **rm** command removes unwanted files so you can clean up your directory tree. The syntax is simple:

> **rm** *filename*

*rem*oves the file called *filename*, as shown in the following examples:

```
$ ls -x
chap10         chap2          chap5          chap9
chapla.old     chap3.old      chap6          haha
chaplb         chap4          chap7
$ rm chap10
$ rm *.old
$ ls -x
chaplb         chap4          chap6          chap9
chap2          chap5          chap7          haha
$ rm ch*
$ ls
haha
$
```

Make sure you are deleting the correct files when you use wildcards in the **rm** command. If you accidentally remove a file you need, you cannot recover it unless you have a backup copy in another directory, or on tape. If you do not have a backup copy of a file you remove with the **rm** command, you will not be able to recover the file at all.

Do not type "rm *" heedlessly. If you do, you will delete all the files in your current working directory. It is good practice to list the files with **ls** * before you remove them. Or, you can use the *-i* option of **rm** which will prompt you *i*nteractively to confirm for each filename that you want it removed.

---

rmdir

Just as you can create new directories, you can also remove them with the **rmdir** command. As a precaution, the **rmdir** command only lets you delete directories that do not contain any files.

The syntax of the command is:

>**rmdir** *dirname*

If a directory you try to remove does contain files, you will get a message like "**rmdir:***dirname* **not empty**".

The procedure for deleting a directory that contains some files is:

1.   Enter **cd** *filename* to get into the directory you want to delete.
2.   Enter **rm *** to remove all files in that directory.
3.   Enter **cd ..** to go to the parent directory.
4.   Enter **rmdir** *filename* to remove the unwanted directory.
5.   Enter **ls -l** to check if the directory was actually removed.

√   *I still get the message "dirname* **not empty**" *even after I've deleted all the files.*

Use **ls -a** to check that there are no hidden files (names beginning with a period) other than . and .. (the current directory and its parent). To remove all hidden files, type **rm .***.

Using **mkdir** and **rmdir**, you can build and remodel your own file hierarchy.

Printing Out Files

By now, it has become a truism that computers will never lead to a paperless office. They make it easier than ever to create a blizzard of paper.

There are two parts to printing: formatting, and actual printing. If you are using a word processor, formatting is generally considered a phase of editing. If you are using a text editor, formatting is a phase of printing.

UNIX includes two very powerful text formatters called **nroff** and **troff**. They are much too complex to describe here. However, before we take up printing proper, let's take a look at a simple formatting program called **pr**.

pr

The **pr** command provides minor formatting of files on the terminal screen or for a printer. For example, if you have a long list of names in a file, you can format it on-screen so that two or more columns of names are produced for readability.

The syntax is:

    pr *file*

pr changes the format of the file only on the screen or on the printed copy and leaves the original file format the same. There are three very useful options of **pr** shown below.

Table 4-1
Useful Options of pr

Option	Description
-k	Produces *k* columns of output
-d	Double-spaces the output
-h *"header"*	Takes the next item as a report *header*

Other options allow you to specify the width of the columns, set the page length, and so on. To see how **pr** works, let's process the file named *food*. Its contents are shown just as they appear in the file.

```
Sweet Tooth
Bangkok Wok
Mandalay
Afghani Cuisine
Isle of Java
Big Apple Deli
Sushi and Sashimi
Tio Pepe's Peppers
```

Using **pr** options, we will specify a two-column report with the header "Restaurants."

```
$ pr -2h "Restaurants" food
Nov 7  09:58 1986  Restaurants               Page 1


Sweet Tooth                    Isle of Java
Bangkok Wok                    Big Apple Deli
Mandalay                       Sushi and Sashimi
Afghani Cuisine                Tio Pepe's Peppers
                          .
                          .
                          .
$
```

The output is separated into pages with the date and time, header (or name of the file, if header is not supplied), and page number. To send this output to the printer instead of the terminal screen, you have to create a *pipe* to the printer program, **lp**. Pipes are discussed in Chapter 5, and **lp** is described in the next section.

lp

If you have a long file, it may be best to get a hard copy of the file so you can view the printed file on paper from top to bottom. The command **lp** is used to print a hardcopy of a file. (On Berkeley systems the equivalent command is called **lpr**). The format is as follows:

    lp *file1 file2* ...

Your System Administrator has probably set up a default printer at your site. To print a file on the default device, use the **lp** command as in the example below. **lp** prints a unique *id* that can be used to cancel the printing request or to check its status.

```
$ lp bills
request id is laserp-525 (1 file)
$
```

The file *bills* will be sent to a printer called *laserp*. The id number of the request is "laserp-525."

lp has several options. Three of the more useful ones are given below.

Table 4-2
Useful Options of lp

Option	Description
-d*printer*	Use given *printer* name, if there is more than one printer at your site. The printer names are assigned by the System Administrator.
-n#	Print # copies of the file
-m	Notify sender when the printing is done

If **lp** does not work at your site, ask other users for the appropriate printer command, and for the printer locations, so you know where to pick up your output.

Problem Checklist

√ *My printout has not come out.*

- Check to see if the printer is currently printing. If it is, other users may have made a request to the same printer ahead of you and your file should be printed in turn. See Chapter 6 for information on how to check the status of your print job.

- If no file is printing, check the physical connections and that the printer is turned ON. The printer may also be hung. Ask your System Administrator for the proper action.

Exercise: Manipulating Files

In this exercise, you will experience creating, renaming and deleting files. Find out if your site has one or more printers and the appropriate command to use for printing.

Copy distant file to working directory	Enter **cp /etc/passwd myfile**
Create new directory	Enter **mkdir temp**
Move file to new directory	Enter **mv myfile temp**
Change working directory	Enter **cd temp**
Copy file to working directory	Enter **cp myfile myfile.two**
Print the file using **lp**	Enter **lp myfile**
List filenames with metacharacter	Enter **ls myfile***
Remove files	Enter **rm myfile***
Go up to parent directory	Enter **cd ..**
Remove a directory	Enter **rmdir temp**
Verify that directory was removed.	Enter **ls -l**

5
Redirecting I/O

Standard Input and Standard Output

A UNIX command usually requires some input (such as a file) and results in output.

In general, if no filename is specified in a command, the shell takes whatever you type in your keyboard as input to the command. Your terminal keyboard is the *standard input*.

When a command has finished running, the results are usually displayed on your terminal screen. The terminal screen is the *standard output*. By default, each command takes its input from the standard input and sends the results to the standard output.

These two default cases of input/output can be varied. You can often use a given file as input to a command using the "<" operator. You can also write the results of a command to a named file or some other device instead of displaying it on the screen using the ">" operator. This is called *input/output redirection*.

Input/output redirection is one of the nicest features of UNIX because of its tremendous power and flexibility.

Putting Text in a File

Instead of always directing the output of a command to the screen, you can redirect output into a file. This is useful when you have a lot of output that would be difficult to read on the screen or when you put files together to create a bigger file. As we've seen, the **cat** command can be used for displaying a short file. It can also be used to put text into a file, or to create a bigger file out of smaller files.

The > Operator

When you append the notation "> *filename*" to the end of a command, the results of the command are diverted from the standard output to the named file. The > symbol is known as the *output redirection operator*.

When you use **cat** with this operator, the contents of the file that are normally displayed on the standard output are diverted into a new file. This becomes clear in the example below.

```
$ cat /etc/passwd > password
$ cat password
root::0:0:Root:/:/bin/sh
daemon:NONE:1:1:Admin:/:
          .
          .
          .
john::128:50:John Doe:/usr/john:/bin/sh
$
```

In the previous example, "**cat /etc/passwd**" simply displayed the file */etc/passwd* on the screen. In the example above, we use the > operator. Instead of printing the results of the command on the terminal screen, the contents are diverted to a file called *password* in the current directory. Listing the contents of the file *password* shows that its contents are the same as the file */etc/passwd*. The effect is the same as the copy command "**cp /etc/passwd password.**"

The > redirection operator can be used with any command, not just with **cat**. For example:

Learning the UNIX Operating System

```
$ who > users
$ date > today
$ ls
today          users          ...
```

You have sent the output of **who** to a file called *users* and the output of **date** to a file called *today*. When you list your directory, you see that two new files have been created: *users* and *today*. Look at these files to see the output produced by the commands **who** and **date**.

```
$ cat users
tim        tty1      Aug 14      07:30
grace      tty2      Aug 14      09:47
john       tty4      Aug 14      08:26
linda      tty7      Aug 14      10:18
$ cat today
Thur  Aug 14   14:36   EDT   1986
$
```

You can also create a small text file using the **cat** command and the > operator. We told you earlier to press CTRL-D if you accidentally type **cat** without a filename. This is because the **cat** command alone takes whatever you type on the keyboard as input. Thus, the command

   cat > *filename*

takes input from the keyboard and redirects it to a file. You can try out the example below:

```
$ cat > goodman
Now is the time for all good men to come to the
aid of their country.
^D
$
```

cat takes the text that you typed as input, and the > operator redirects it to a file called *goodmen*. Type CTRL-D on a new line by itself to signal the end of the text. You should get back the system prompt.

You can also create a bigger file out of many smaller files using the **cat** command and the ">" operator. The form:

   cat *file1 file2* > *newfile*

creates a file *newfile*, consisting of *file2* appended to *file1*.

```
$ cat today goodmen > fortune
$ cat fortune
Thur   Aug 14   14:36   EDT   1986
Now is the time for all good men to come to the
aid of their country.
$
```

The >> Operator

You can also append information to the end of an existing file, instead
of replacing its contents, by using the >> (*append redirection*) operator in place of the > (*output redirection*) operator.

> **cat** *file2* >> *file1*

appends the contents of *file2* to the end of *file1*.

```
$ cat users >> fortune
$ cat fortune
Thur   Aug 14   14:36   EDT   1986
Now is the time for all good men to come to the
aid of their country.
tim        tty1   Aug 14   07:30
grace      tty2   Aug 14   09:47
john       tty4   Aug 14   08:26
linda      tty7   Aug 14   10:18
$
```

If you are using the > (*output redirection*) operator, you should be
careful not to accidentally overwrite the contents of a file. Your system may let you redirect output to an existing file. If so, the old file
will be deleted (or, in UNIX lingo, "clobbered"). It is your own
responsibility to be careful not to overwrite a much-needed file. If
you are using the C shell, there is a mechanism to protect you from
the risk of overwriting an important file. If you set the "noclobber"
variable, the C shell will not let you redirect onto an existing file and
overwrite its contents.

Pipes and Filters

In addition to redirecting input/output to a named file, you can connect two commands together so that the output from one program becomes the input of the next command. Two or more commands connected in this way form a *pipe*. A pipe is designated by a vertical bar (I) on the command line between two commands. When a pipe is set up between two commands, the standard output of the command to the left of the pipe symbol becomes the standard input of the command to the right of the pipe symbol. Any two programs can form a pipe as long as the first program writes to standard output and the second program reads from standard input.

When a program takes its input from another program, performs some operation on that input, and writes the result to the standard output (or possibly pipes the result to yet another program), it is referred to as a *filter*. One of the most common uses of filters is to modify output. Just as a common filter culls out unwanted items, the UNIX filters can be used to restructure output so that only the desired lines are displayed on the screen or sent to another file.

Almost **all** UNIX commands can be used to form pipes. Some programs that are commonly used as filters are described below. Note that these programs are **not** used only as filters or parts of pipes. They are useful as individual commands.

grep

grep is a very useful program that searches a file or files for lines which contain strings of a certain pattern. The syntax is:

grep *"pattern" file*

The name "grep" derives from the **ed** (a UNIX line editor) command **g/re/p** which means "*g*lobally search for a *re*gular *e*xpression and *p*rint all lines containing it". A regular expression combines a string of text with some special characters used for pattern matching. When you learn more about text editing, you can use regular expressions to specify complex patterns of text.

The simplest use of **grep** is to look for a pattern consisting of a fixed character string. For example, it can be used in a pipe so that only those lines of the input files containing a given string are sent to the standard output.

```
$ ls -l | grep "Aug"
-rw-rw-rw-   1 john     doc      11008 Aug  6 14:10 ch02
-rw-rw-r--   1 john     doc      14827 Aug  9 12:40 ch03
-rw-rw-rw-   1 john     doc       8515 Aug  6 15:30 ch07
-rw-rw-r--   1 john     doc       2488 Aug 15 10:51 intro
$
```

The simple pipe in our example looks for all files in your directory that contain the string "Aug" (that is, they were last modified in August) and sends those lines to the terminal screen.

grep has a number of options that allow you to modify the search. Some of these are given in the table below.

Table 5-1
Useful grep Options

Option	Description
-v	Print all lines that do not match pattern
-n	Print the matched line and its line number
-l	Print only the names of files with matching lines (letter "l")
-c	Print only the *c*ount of matching lines
-i	Ignore upper and lower case

sort

The **sort** program arranges the contents of a file alphabetically or numerically. The simple example below sorts the first field or column of the file called *food* (which we have seen earlier) alphabetically.

```
$ sort food
Afghani Cuisine
Bangkok Wok
```

```
Big Apple Deli
Isle of Java
Mandalay
Sushi and Sashimi
Sweet Tooth
Tio Pepe's Peppers
```

sort arranges lines of text alphabetically by default. There are many options that control the sort order. Some of these are given in the table below.

Table 5-2
Useful sort Options

Option	Description
-n	Sort by arithmetic value, ignoring blanks and tabs
-r	Reverse the order of sort
f	Sort regardless of upper or lower case
+x	Limit sort to field x

More than two commands may be linked up into a pipe. Taking the previous pipe example using **grep**, we can further sort the files modified in August by order of size. The following pipe consists of the commands **ls, grep** and **sort**:

```
$ ls -l | grep "Aug" | sort +4n
-rw-rw-r--  1 carol   doc    1605 Aug 23 07:35 macros
-rw-rw-r--  1 john    doc    2488 Aug 15 10:51 intro
-rw-rw-rw-  1 john    doc    8515 Aug  6 15:30 ch07
-rw-rw-rw-  1 john    doc   11008 Aug  6 14:10 ch02
-rw-rw-r--  1 john    doc   14827 Aug  9 12:40 ch03
$
```

This pipe sorts all files in your directory modified in August by order of size, and prints them to the terminal screen. The **sort** option *+4n* tells UNIX to skip four fields (a field is preceded by a blank) then sort the lines in *n*umeric order. Both **grep** and **sort** are used here as filters to modify the output of the **ls -l** command.

pg

The **pg** program that you saw earlier can also be used as a filter. A long output would normally zip by you on the screen but if you run a file through **pg** as a filter, the screen fills up with one screenful of text at a time.

Let us assume in our example that you have a long directory listing. To make reading the sorted file more manageable, send the output through **pg**:

```
$ ls -l | grep "Aug" | sort +4n | pg

-rw-rw-r--   1 carol   doc     1605 Aug 23 07:35 macros
-rw-rw-r--   1 john    doc     2488 Aug 15 10:51 intro
-rw-rw-rw-   1 john    doc     8515 Aug  6 15:30 ch07
-rw-rw-rw-   1 john    doc    11008 Aug  6 14:10 ch02
-rw-rw-r--   1 john    doc    14827 Aug  9 12:40 ch03
                                .
                                .
                                .
-rw-rw-rw-   1 john    doc    16867 Aug  6 15:56 ch05
:
```

The screen will fill up with one screenful of text consisting of lines sorted by order of file size. The colon at the bottom of the screen prompts you for the **pg** command to move forward or backward in the sorted file. To continue reading the file, you can press any of the keys as described earlier in the discussion of the **pg** program.

Exercise: Redirecting Input/Output

The following exercises show you how to redirect output, create a simple pipe, and use filters to modify output.

Redirect output to a file	Enter **who > users**
Sort output of a command	Enter **who | sort**
Append sorted output to a file	Enter **who | sort >> users**
Display output to screen	Enter **pg users**
Display long output to screen	Enter **ls -l /bin | pg**

6
Multi-Tasking

Getting More Than One Job Done

Suppose you are running a command that will take a long time to process. On a single-tasking system like MS-DOS, you would enter the command and then wait for the system prompt telling you that you could enter a new command. In UNIX, however, there is a way to enter new commands in the "foreground" while one or more commands are still running in the "background." This is called *background processing*. Background processing is useful for running slow programs whose output you do not need immediately.

When you enter a command as a background process, the shell assigns a process ID to the background process and prints out the process ID. The system prompt reappears immediately so that you can enter a new command. The command is still running in the "background" but you can use the system to do other things during that time. You can also log off at this time since the background process runs to completion even when you are not using the system.

Running a Command in the Background

Running a command as a background process is most often done to free up a terminal when you know that the command will take a long time to run.

To run a command as a background process, add the "&" character at the end of the command line before you press the RETURN key. This is shown in the example below:

```
$ nroff -ms chap1 > chap1.out &
[1] 29890
$
```

(**nroff** is a program used to format documents for printing. It is used here as an example because text formatting usually takes a while, and is an ideal candidate for background processing. See your UNIX documentation for details on **nroff**.)

The process ID (PID) for the command is 29890. The process ID is useful when you want to check the status of a background process or to cancel it when you have to. You don't need to remember the process ID, since there is a UNIX command (explained below) to check on what processes you have running. In the C shell, a line showing the status of the command will be printed on your screen when the background process is complete.

In the C shell, you can put an entire sequence of commands separated by semicolons into the background by putting an & at the end of the entire command line. In the Bourne shell, you need to enclose the command sequence in parentheses before typing the ampersand:

(command1; command2)&

On Berkeley UNIX systems, the C shell supports an additional feature called job control. You can use the *suspend character* (usually CTRL-Z) to suspend a program running in the foreground. The program will pause, and the shell will give you a new system prompt. You can then do anything else you like, including putting the suspended program into the background using the **bg** command. The **fg** command will bring a background process to the foreground.

Checking on a Process

If you find that a background process is taking too long to execute, or you change your mind and want to stop a process, you can check the status of the process and even cancel it if it is no longer wanted.

ps

When you enter the single-word command **ps**, you can see how long a process has been running. The output of **ps** also tells you the process ID of the background process and the terminal from which it was run.

```
$ ps
 PID   TTY   TIME      COMMAND
 8048  020   0:12  sh
 8699  020   0:02  ps
  |     |     |
  | terminal |
  |   line   |
  |          |
process      run
   id        time

$
```

In its basic form, **ps** lists the following:

process ID   A unique number assigned by UNIX to the background process.

terminal line   The terminal number from which the background process was sent.

run time   The amount of computer time (in minutes and seconds) that the process has used.

command   The name of the process.

At the very least, **ps** will list two processes: the shell (**sh** or **csh**) and **ps** itself. You should also see the names of any other programs you have run in the background.

You should be aware that there are two types of programs on UNIX systems, compiled programs and shell scripts. Shell scripts are sequences of stored commands. If you execute a shell script in the background, you will see an additional **sh** (or **csh**) command in the **ps** listing, plus all of the commands that are executed by the shell script. You *won't* see the name of the command you typed.

On Berkeley systems with job control, the C shell includes a command called **jobs**, which lists all background processes. As mentioned above, there are commands to change the foreground/background status of jobs. There are other job control commands as well. See your UNIX documentation for details.

Stopping a Process

You realize, after some time, that you have made a mistake in putting a process in the background. Or, after checking on the status of the process, you decide that it is taking too long to execute. You can cancel a background process if you know its process ID.

kill

The **kill** command is used to stop a background process from being executed further. The format of the command is:

> **kill** *PID(s)*

kill terminates the designated process IDs (shown under the PID heading in the **ps** listing). If you do not know the process ID, do a **ps** first to display the status of background processes.

In the following example, the **sleep** command simply causes a process to "go to sleep" for *n* number of seconds. We enter two commands, **sleep** and **who**, on the same line as a background process.

```
$ (sleep 60; who)&
[1]   21087
$ ps
 PID    TTY    TIME    COMMAND
20055    4     0:10    sh
21088    4     0:00    sleep
```

```
 21089    4      0:02     ps
$ kill 21088
Terminated
tom      tty2    Aug 30   11:27
grace    tty4    Aug 30   12:24
tim      tty5    Aug 30   07:52
dale     tty7    Aug 30   14:34
```

Suppose we decide that 60 seconds is too long a time to wait for the output of **who**. The **ps** listing shows that **sleep** has the process ID number 21088 so we use this PID to kill the **sleep** process. You will see the message: "**Terminated**." The **who** command is executed immediately, since it is no longer waiting on **sleep**, and proceeds to list the users logged into the system.

Problem Checklist

√ *The process didn't die when I told it to.*

Some processes can be hard to kill. If a normal **kill** of these processes is not working, enter "**kill -9** *PID*." This is a sure kill and can destroy anything, including the command shell which is interpreting it.

In addition, if you've run a shell script, killing the **sh** which got it all started will not automatically kill all dependent processes. You must kill them independently. However, killing a process that is feeding data into a pipe will generally also kill any processes receiving that data.

Spooling

The printer on your UNIX system is usually shared by a group of UNIX users. *Spooling* is a method of keeping track of print jobs and sending them to a printer one at a time.

When you enter the **lp** command to print a file, the system prompt returns to the screen and you can enter another command. However, that does not mean that your file has been printed. Your file has been spooled on the printer queue and if there are no other print jobs, then yours will be printed. Spooling is a form of background processing since You can enter new commands while your files are queued up for printing in the background.

Viewing the Printer Queue

You will usually be given a message to inform you when your file has been printed. If you're impatient, and want to find out how many files are ahead of you in the printer queue, you can use the **lpstat** command. The **cancel** command allows you to terminate a printing request made by **lp**. (The equivalent Berkeley commands are **lpq** to show the status of the queue, and **lprm** to remove a print request. See your documentation for details.)

lpstat

The **lpstat** command displays the contents of the printer queue. **lpstat** shows the request id, the owner, the size of the files, when it was sent for printing, and the status of the request, in that order. Use **lpstat -o** if you want to see all output requests rather than just your own. Requests are shown in the order that they will be printed.

```
$ lpstat -o
laserp-573  john   128865  Nov 7  11:27  on laserp
laserp-574  grace  82744   Nov 7  11:28
laserp-575  john   23347   Nov 7  11:35
$
```

The first entry shows that the request "laserp-573" is currently printing on *laserp*. The exact format and amount of information given about the printer queue may differ from system to system. If the printer queue is empty, **lpstat** will say "**No entries**" or simply give you back the system prompt.

cancel

cancel is used to terminate a printing request that was sent using the
lp command. You can specify either the *id* of the request (printed by
lp) or the name of the printer.

When you want to cancel a request, list the status of the printer queue
with **lpstat**, then invoke the **cancel** command.

```
$ lpstat
laserp-573   john   128865   Nov 7   11:27 on laserp
laserp-574   grace   82744   Nov 7   11:28
laserp-575   john    23347   Nov 7   11:35
$ cancel laserp-575
request "laserp-575" canceled
$
```

Specifying the request id cancels the request, even if it is currently
printing.

To cancel whatever request is currently printing, regardless of its id,
simply type cancel and the printer name:

```
$ cancel laserp
request "laserp-573" cancelled
```

7
Where to Go From Here

Standard UNIX Documentation

Now that you have reached the end of this learning guide, you should be able to go through a typical UNIX session with ease. At this point, you are possibly eager to know the various options to the commands that were introduced and the many other commands available in UNIX. You are ready to consult the documentation for your system.

UNIX documentation has been remolded into many guises in the hands of different system manufacturers. However, almost all UNIX documentation is derived from a manual originally called the *UNIX Programmer's Manual*.

At one point, the *UNIX Programmer's Manual* was divided into two heavy volumes: Volume 1 and Volume 2. Volume 1 contained individual reference pages for each available command. Volume 2 contained tutorial articles on many (but far from all) of the more important commands.

In its earlier incarnation, Volume 1 was divided into the following sections:

Section 1   General UNIX commands and application programs

Section 2   UNIX system calls

Section 3   Standard subroutine libraries for input /output, mathematical functions, Fortran 77, and specialized subroutines

Section 4	File formats
Section 5	Miscellaneous facilities such as character set tables, macro packages, and so on
Section 6	Games
Section 7	Special files.
Section 8	Administrative commands.

Berkeley UNIX has maintained this original organization, though the number and the size of the volumes has grown. AT&T's System V (Release 2 and 3) has divided the old Volume 2 into a great many separate guides (tutorials), and has written much new tutorial material. Section 1 of the old Volume 1, the alphabetical command reference, is called the *User Reference Manual*.

This is probably the most important of all the manuals, since it lists all the options to all the commands you can enter on the command line.

Online Documentation

Many UNIX installations (especially larger systems with plenty of disk space) have Volume 1 of the *UNIX Programmer's Manual* stored on the computer and made available online to UNIX users.

If you want some information about the correct syntax for entering a command or the particular features of a program, enter the command **man** and the name of the command. The format is:

man *command*

For example, if you want to find information about the program **mail**, which allows you to send messages to other users, you would type:

```
$ man mail
   .
   .
   .
$
```

The output of **man** is implicitly filtered through the **more** command.

After you type in the command, the screen will fill up with text. Press the ⌈SPACE BAR⌋ key to go on to the next screen. As in the **more** command, you will not be able to go back and read previous screens.

Berkeley UNIX systems also have a command called **apropos** to help you locate a command if you have an idea of what it does but are not sure of its correct name. Type **apropos** followed by a descriptive phrase, and a list of possibly relevant commands will be displayed.

Interesting Things to Learn

Out of the hundreds of UNIX commands that have been developed, the commands for editing files are probably among the first that you should learn. As you get more familiar with other UNIX commands, you can customize your working environment and also create commands for your own special functions.

Editors

Word processing is one of the most frequently used functions of a computer. Whether you are writing a computer program or a chapter of a novel, basic editing is sure to be the first step.

It will help you become more productive if you devote some time to learning the UNIX editor on your system. This is usually the line editor **ed** or the screen editors **vi** and **emacs**. Screen editors allow you to move the cursor anywhere on the screen and edit characters or lines simply by typing at the current cursor position. **emacs** is another screen editor that is gaining a significant following.

Whether you use **ed, vi** or **emacs**, you will have to learn the special commands associated with the editor that will allow you to search, add and delete characters or lines. You will find that some commands come more easily to you than others. Do not be concerned with learning all the commands. Use those which you are more comfortable with and will help you get the work done.

Shell Programming

We have mentioned earlier that the shell is the system's command interpreter. It reads each command you enter at your terminal and performs the operation that you called for. The System Administrator decides the type of shell that runs when you log in to your account.

The shell is just an ordinary program that can be called by a UNIX command. However, it contains some features (like variables, control structures, subroutines, and so on) that make it very similar to a programming language. You can save a series of shell commands in a file, called a shell script, to accomplish specialized functions.

Programming the shell should only be attempted when you are reasonably confident of your ability to use UNIX commands. UNIX is quite a powerful tool and its capabilities become more apparent when you try your hand at shell programming.

Take the time to learn the basics. Then, when you're faced with a new task, take the time to browse through the reference manual to find which programs or options will help you get the job done more easily. Once you've done that, learn how to build shell scripts so that you never have to type a complicated command sequence more than once.

Quick Reference

Terms

Home Directory - The directory assigned to your account. When you log in, you are in this directory.

Login ID - Your name or initials, used to identify yourself to the login prompt. Also called "user ID" or UID.

Pathname - The address of a file or directory on the file system. An *absolute* or full pathname specifies how to get there from the root directory. A *relative* pathname specifies how to get there from the current working directory.

Parent Directory - In the tree directory, this is the directory at the next higher level. ".." indicates the parent directory above the current working directory.

Pipe - A pipe sends the output of one command on to become the input of the next command. Often used with a *filter* to modify or limit output.

Process - A program that is being executed by the computer. *PID* is the ID number assigned to each process.

Shell - The shell interprets commands before presenting them to the operating system for execution. There are different shells available; two of the most popular are the Bourne shell and the C-shell.

Working Directory - Your current directory or location on the file system.

Commands and Their Meanings

Command	Description
cat *files*	Concatenate one file to another and display
cd	Change to home directory
cd *pathname*	Change working directory to *pathname*
cp *old new*	Copy *old* file to *new* file
date	Display current date and time
grep *pattern file*	Show lines matching *pattern* in *file*
kill *PID*	End background process *PID*
lp *file*	Send *file* to default printer
lpq *file*	Check on requests on printer queue (Berkeley)
lpr *file*	Send *file* to printer (Berkeley)
lprm *request*	Cancel a print request (Berkeley)
lpstat	Check on requests on printer queue
ls	List names of files in current directory
ln *file new*	Create link *new* name to *file* name
mail	Read your own mail
mail *user*	Send mail to person with *user* name
man *command*	Display manual page of *command*
mkdir *pathname*	Create a new directory with *pathname*
more *file*	Display *file* to fill screen
mv *file new*	Move or rename *old* file to *new* file
pg *file*	Display one screenful of *file* at a time
ps	List current processes and their PIDs
pwd	Print working directory
rm *file*	Remove or erase *file*
rmdir *pathname*	Remove empty directory with *pathname*
sort *file*	Sort lines of *file*
who	List users currently on system
who am i	Display listing for this account

Special Symbols

Symbol	Description
|	To set up a pipe
>	To redirect output to a file
<	To redirect input from a file
>>	To append output to an existing file
/	Separator used in pathnames
&	To process command in the background
*	To match any number of characters in filename
?	To match any single character in filename
[ ]	To match any one of the enclosed characters in filename.

Index

standard output 49
stopping a process 61
stty command 34-35
suspend character 59
syntax of UNIX commands 13
System V 2

T
troff command 45

U
umask command 34-35
unresponsive terminal 15-16
user id 69

V
vi editor 36

W
who command 10, 61, 70
wildcards 37-39
    danger of using with **rm** 43
working directory 21, 40, 69

Colophon

Our look is the result of reader comments, our own experimentation, and distribution channels.

Distinctive covers complement our distinctive approach to UNIX documentation, breathing personality and life into potentially dry subjects. UNIX and its attendant programs can be unruly beasts. Nutshell Handbooks help you tame them.

The animals featured on the cover of *Learning the UNIX Operating System* is the horned owl. The horned owl is the most powerful of the North American owls, measuring from 18 to 25 inches long. This nocturnal bird of prey feeds exclusively on animals—primarily rabbits, rodents, and birds, including other owls—which it locates by sound rather than sight, its night vision being little better than ours. To aid in its hunting, an owl has soft feathers which muffle the sound of its motion, making it virtually silent in flight. A tree-dwelling bird, it generally chooses to inhabit the old nests of other large birds such as hawks and crows rather than build its own nest.

Edic Freedman designed this cover and the entire UNIX bestiary that appears on other Nutshell Handbooks. The beasts themselves are adapted from 19th-century engravings from the Dover Pictorial Archive.

The text of this book is set in Times Roman; headings are Helvetica; examples are Courier. Text was prepared using SoftQuad's *sqtroff* text formatter. Printing is done on an Apple LaserWriter.